language
of
forgiveness

learn it • live it • love it

quinn schipper

NEW FORUMS
Stillwater, Oklahoma
U.S.A.

NEW FORUMS PRESS INC.

Published in the United States of America
by New Forums Press, Inc.1018 S. Lewis St.
Stillwater, OK 74074
www.newforums.com

Copyright © 2009 by Quinn Schipper.

All rights reserved. No part of this publication may be reproduced or transmitted in any form or by any means, electronic or mechanical, including photocopy, or any information storage or retrieval system, without permission in writing from the publisher.

Library of Congress Cataloging-in-Publication Data Pending

This book may be ordered in bulk quantities at discount from New Forums Press, Inc., P.O. Box 876, Stillwater, OK 74076 [Federal I.D. No. 73 1123239]. Printed in the United States of America.

ISBN 10: 1-58107-163-9
ISBN 13: 978-1-581071-63-4

Unless otherwise noted, Scripture quotations are from the New Living Translation of the Holy Bible copyright © 1996, 2004 by Tyndale House Publishers. All rights reserved.

Contents

1. The Landscape of Forgiveness / 6
2. The Lord of Forgiveness / 14
3. The Law of Forgiveness / 21
4. The Lure of Forgiveness / 29
5. The Language of Forgiveness / 37
6. The Lifestyle of Forgiveness / 47

Foreword

I was delighted to be asked to preview Quinn's new book on forgiveness. Many of us have fallen into the trap of believing that we just need to "forget" our pain, "buck up" and move on, or even that our anger towards those who have harmed us finally gives us power over them. Not so! In the years that I have been studying and ministering inner healing, I have found forgiveness to be the essential element of lasting freedom. Thank you, Quinn, for compiling an insightful, concise teaching that many will find helpful in holding onto their own freedom as well as helping to set other captives free.

Dawna De Silva
Founder of Sozo Ministry
Bethel Church
Redding, California

Introduction

I was 20 years old when I first stood at the South Rim of the Grand Canyon. A friend and I had arrived the night before and pitched our tent in the darkness. When I crawled out at daybreak, I was mesmerized by the spectacular vista as brilliant hues of dawn lit the expanse. The vast depth and breadth appeared to be of impossible scale.

The "doorway of forgiveness" is a supernatural portal to pass through in order to be released of resentment, bitterness, and offense. To some, merely opening that door might be similar to my first daunting sight of the Grand Canyon. Even the very thought of crossing from one side to the other seems incomprehensible.

Many people are embittered because of things that have been either said or done to them, or perhaps by things that have not been said or done. Consequently, they become imprisoned by unforgiveness and may not even realize it.

The fact is, people will hurt us. The truth is, we can forgive them, even as we have been forgiven. I invite you to cross the threshold and discover God's redemptive work and how the language of forgiveness brings freedom.

The Landscape of Forgiveness

In October 2006, an Amish community in rural Pennsylvania was rocked when five of their young girls in a schoolhouse were shot and killed by a man who then turned his gun on himself. America was astonished as the Amish people's response was to extend forgiveness to the man's family.

Forgiveness is best addressed in a safe environment of community and relationship. There is usually plenty of company to be found in our hurt and anger, but we are often alone on the pathways that lead to forgiveness. Retribution seems so natural to us. By contrast, redemption is supernatural. In the case of the Amish massacre, the community helped absorb the hurt as they sought to deal expediently and redemptively to forgive the atrocity.

People are more likely to forgive if an offense is minor, if the offender apologizes, or if the offense occurs in a committed relationship. However, the common inclinations of those who harbor unforgiveness are anger, bitterness, and seeking revenge – even if limited to mental overtures that are never acted upon. After all, if we do not make plans to get even, how will justice get accomplished?

Consequently, the lie is embraced, "It is my responsibility to keep the offense alive until justice is served." The truth, however, is found in Romans 12:19: *"Dear friends, never take revenge. Leave that to the righteous anger of God. For the Scriptures say, 'I will take revenge; (I will pay them back,' says the Lord."* (Deuteronomy 32:35)

Furthermore, people tend to rationalize their attitude and behavior regarding unforgiveness:

"After what she did to me? No way! I will never forgive her!"

"How could I ever forgive myself for what I caused?"

"How can God possibly forgive me for that? I don't deserve to be forgiven."

We are not well educated about forgiveness. Many are devoid of forgiveness experiences or examples by others. Our culture of entitlement works against forgiveness. People are typically ignorant of what forgiveness really means. Some have never experienced it.

The word "forgive" simply means "to let go." I liken this definition to a helium balloon. If you were able to write on a balloon all the offenses incurred by another, how large of a balloon would you need? More than one person has replied to me, "A hot air balloon!"

Another picture of forgiveness is that of a canceled debt. When I take stock of my sin against God, instead of my having to pay the debt of what I owe him, he dismisses it and stamps it "Paid in Full." He requires me to do likewise with others and even helps me to do so. Romans 13:8 says, *"Let no debt remain outstanding, except the continuing debt to love one another."* (NIV)

Defining forgiveness

When it comes to offenses, many of us are like elephants – we never forget! Although to "forgive and forget" is a popular adage, it is abnormal, if not undesirable, to forget.

Many thoughts distort our understanding of true forgiveness, often making us confuse it with what it most certainly is not. Let us look at several frequent misunderstandings...

Forgiveness is not the same as:

1) Forgetting... It is impossible and unrealistic to forget significant life events, unless deep trauma has caused an amnesic condition. Forgiveness does not change our memories, history, or humanity. Real offenses actually occurred. Therefore, forgiving and remembering are closely linked: we need to remember in order to forgive. Forgiveness does not mean we forget what took place; it simply initiates God's redemption and changes our perspective.

   Hebrews 8:12 says, *"And I will forgive their wickedness, and I will never again remember their sins."* God forgives ... he does not forget. Instead, he chooses not to dwell on offenses or remind himself of them.

   As a pastor, I have forfeited what might otherwise have been some really great sermon illustrations by forgiving my son of childhood offenses. Furthermore, each pardon came with the spoken commitment not to bring the matter back to remembrance, to hold it against him, or to speak of it with anyone else. I chose to cancel the debt and remind neither him nor myself of the forgiven offense. 1 Corinthians 13:5 affirms that love *"keeps no record of being wronged."*

2) Grieving... Feeling pain does not mean you have not forgiven. Grieving is a normal response to loss and is a process that takes time. It is permissible and reasonable to grieve over

something that cannot be recovered. It could be that residual pain is not that of the original offense, but of unexpressed grief associated with it. Matthew 5:4 reassures that *"God blesses those who mourn, for they will be comforted."*

3) Trust... An offense often shatters trust. Forgiveness and trust are not the same. Forgiveness does not instantly reinstate trust or let the other person off the hook scot-free. Neither does it cover another's repeated offenses.

4) Restoration... When a person wrongfully collided with my nephew's pride-and-joy Mustang, his response of forgiveness did not immediately restore the extensive damage to his car or resolve other complications associated with the accident. When there is a relational collision, it may not be possible or desirable to restore the relationship. However, forgiving the other person releases you of bitterness as well as any guilt or shame if the relationship cannot continue.

5) Reconciliation... Reconciliation implies both the participation and agreement of two parties. Just because we forgive does not mean we are agreeing with what happened. Although reconciliation can be the outcome of forgiveness, in some cases it may be improbable. Nevertheless, reconciliation needs to be linked to responsibility.

6) Correction... Forgiveness and correction can work in tandem. This may require confronting another person in order to forgive him and to set things right. Luke 17:3 explains, *"If another believer sins, rebuke that person; then if there is repentance, forgive."*

7) Approval... When Jesus forgave the woman caught in adultery (John 8) he neither approved of her wrongdoing nor condemned her. Rather, he advised her to go and leave her life of sin. He forgave her without siding with her.

8) Denial... The tendency is to detach ourselves from whatever causes pain. Denial becomes an easy way out if the pain is too great to deal with at the conscious level. Repression is typically subconscious and involuntary and may contribute to adverse health issues such as high blood pressure and anxiety. Forgiving others is not denying that we have been wounded or pretending that the offense was no big deal. Denying that others really did hurt us, causing physical, emotional, or mental pain, actually works against the forgiveness process.

9) Avoidance... Avoidance is refusing to take an offense seriously or passing it off as insignificant or of no consequence. God never dismisses our sins as inconsequential, yet he totally forgives. Pretending we are not hurt is a form of both avoidance and denial. Either can become a rationale to evade dealing with forgiveness.

10) Responsibility... Forgiving does not mean that the person committing an offense is not responsible for his behavior. Forgiveness is not justifying or explaining away what a person has done. Some very unfair things happen to us. Seeking to understand does not excuse the sin, inappropriate behavior, or offense, but it may help us acknowledge it realistically and address it responsibly.

Forgiveness does not mean we close our eyes to those who continue to harm us or others. For example, forgiveness does not mean a crime goes unreported. There are times it would be absolutely irresponsible to remain silent or to turn the proverbial blind eye.

11) Punishment... Although a person's action may even be punishable in a court of law, it is not our place to punish. When we forgive, we refuse to punish those we feel deserve it. The nature of penalty is up to God. He does not want or need our help to mete out vengeance. Yielding our will to his will acknowledges that he alone decides what ought to be done.

12) Consequence... We do not escape the consequences of our sins simply because we are forgiven or have forgiven someone else. Even though God forgave David of both adultery (with Uriah's wife, Bathsheba) and murder (of Uriah, her innocent husband), David still suffered the consequences of exposure and shame, the death of his child, family rebellion, generational adultery, and other woes.

Defining offense

All relationships need forgiveness at some point or other. Following a workshop I helped facilitate, I read an evaluation comment pleading, "Quinn, *please* call my wife and let her know it's okay to forgive me."

Unforgiveness is rooted in offense. The word "offense" means "stumbling block; an impediment to belief or understanding; an obstacle to progress." Interestingly, it also means "a cause or occasion of sin." Offenses are common, yet they can provoke us to hold grudges, ponder revenge, ruin others' reputations, and seethe with anger.

The root of offense

Mark 6:1-6 helps us understand the meaning and implications of offense. When Jesus visited his hometown of Nazareth and taught in the synagogue, offense took root among those who heard him. While *"many who heard him were amazed,"* others scoffed, "Who does he think he is?!" or as Mark states it, *"they took offense at him."*

Hebrews 12:15 warns, *"Watch out that no poisonous root of bitterness grows up to trouble you, corrupting many."* A root of bitterness will get established in the soil of offense if it is not dealt with properly and in God's way. Roots absorb, store, and grow. If there is a root of bitterness in a person's life, sooner or later it will shoot to the surface stirring up anger and revenge, poisoning relationships, causing anguish and pain, rehearsing the hurt, and even providing an entry point for demonic infiltration. Once the enemy gets a foothold, he will do everything possible to reinforce and/or replicate the offense, thus compounding the bitterness. Bitter people struggle to recognize their own bitterness. They tend to justify their position, be overly critical, and may secretly celebrate the misfortune of others.

When we had a large tree removed from our yard, I requested that the stump be ground well below grade. Nonetheless, shoots still forced their way upward. I would systematically poison the shoots, then cut them off. They persisted in appearing! The tree was gone, the stump ground, and sod masked the spot – but the root system buried deep in the ground would not relent. Somewhere down there, a root still existed with some life in it. So it is with a hidden root of bitterness. The only way to kill that root is with forgiveness. Not forgiving is like swallowing poison yourself then expecting the person with whom you are bitter to get sick.

The fruit of offense

Mark 6 goes on to reveal that not only did Jesus offend many, but also that they refused to believe in him. At least four fruits of offense are found in this passage:

1) Dishonor: *"A prophet is honored everywhere except in his own hometown and among his relatives and his own family."* (v4)

2) Disability: *"He couldn't do any miracles among them except to place his hands on a few sick people and heal them."* (v5)

3) Disbelief: *"And he was amazed at their unbelief."* (v6)

4) Disorder: Offense and unforgiveness can separate us relationally within ourselves, from others, and from the Lord. A corresponding passage in Luke 4:14-30 reveals that the people became so furious they intended to kill Jesus by throwing him over a cliff!

The more we hold on to offenses, the more they grip us. Bitterness produces bad fruit. When bitterness takes root and offense bears fruit, things can turn rotten – sometimes really fast!

If you tend to be critical, bitter, or walk in offense, consider your options. You can retaliate. You can disconnect from the pain. You can stay trapped in uncertainty. Or, you can forgive. Read on!

The Lord of Forgiveness

Jesus suffered indescribable cruelty before ever being nailed to the cross, his merciless scourging so vicious that it disturbs the conscious. The chilling reality is that the soldier assigned to the flogging used a whip of braided leather thongs with metal balls and sharp pieces of bone woven into them. The balls caused deep contusions while the bone shards would cut the swollen flesh. The severity of shredding could expose the spine and entrails after tearing away muscle and veins. Many people would die from this kind of beating even before they could be crucified. Survivors would experience excruciating pain and go into hypovolemic shock due to the loss of large volumes of blood. In desperation, the body and any still functioning organs would rally for survival.

Jesus was already in critical condition before the crucifixion, yet he managed to carry his own cross part of the way to Golgatha. Simon of Cyrene was forced to relieve him of it. On site, crude spikes driven through his wrists and ankles not only secured him to the coarse wood but also destroyed the dominant nerves to his extremities. The pain was absolutely unbearable. Once a person was hanging vertically, crucifixion was essentially an agonizingly slow death by asphyxiation culminating in cardiac arrest.

Undeserved humiliation and ridicule bombarded Jesus from the moment of his arrest in Gesthemane until he breathed his last after several hours fastened to the cross. Once he was hoisted into place, the Lord surveyed those who had mercilessly abused and falsely accused him. Then he made one of the most astonishing and redemptive statements of his ministry:

"Father, forgive them, for they don't know what they are doing." (Luke 23:34) As impossible as it may seem to do, this must be our response as well to injustice, abuse, false accusation, insult, and mockery.

Many people are damaged from the cruelty inflicted by others. For example, when an adult violates the boundaries of innocence and abuses a child, neither really has any idea what may be the outcome of that trespass. Often, the injured party dissociates from the pain in order to survive, particularly if the abuse is repeated. In the case of a child who has no means of physical escape from the abuse, the victim mentally distances himself from his abuser and the corresponding pain. All of this creates mental, emotional, physical, and spiritual disconnections that contribute to relational disorder on many levels – including separation from God.

The injustices against Jesus Christ in the brutal events leading to and including his crucifixion are beyond human comprehension. As you come to a place of willingness to forgive your offenders, consider both the suffering and the example of the Lord. Allow him to go with you to the place of pain and, together, express forgiveness of those who have wounded you.

I have thought of what it would mean if God treated me as I treat others when it comes to harboring offenses, nursing bitterness, and refusing forgiveness. That thought begs me to honestly ask, "Do I want those whom I have hurt to forgive me?" That means both those I have unintentionally offended and those I have purposely hurt. My answer is, "Yes!"

True identity

Matthew 9:1-8 tells how once in Jesus' own town, some people brought to him a paralyzed man on a mat. Seeing their faith, Jesus said to the paralyzed man, *"Be encouraged, my child! Your sins are forgiven."* But some of the teachers of religious law took offense at this and said to themselves, *"That's blasphemy! Does he think he's God?"*

Jesus knew what they were thinking, so he asked them, *"Why do you have such evil thoughts in your hearts? Is it easier to say 'Your sins are forgiven,' or 'Stand up and walk'? So I will prove to you that the Son of Man has the authority on earth to forgive sins."* Then Jesus turned to the paralyzed man and said, *"Stand up, pick up your mat, and go home!"*

And the man jumped up and went home! Fear swept through the crowd as they saw this happen. And they praised God for sending a man with such great authority.

In this account, Jesus performs the miracle of physical healing to validate the greater miracle of healing the soul and redeeming a life through forgiven sins. After all, eternal life is of greater importance than temporal physical life. Jesus gave an outward sign – immediate and total healing of paralysis – to verify his authority to forgive sins.

Clearly this man had a problem: he was paralyzed. People did not think of him possibly being any other way except paralyzed and powerless. Many may have known him simply as "the paralytic." Today, wounded people may be paralyzed by a victim mentality linked to unforgiveness. Their issue – maybe anger, bitterness, or fear – has become their identity.

"Identity theft" has become a common term in our culture. It refers to the fraud of someone pretending to be another person in order to take advantage of him or to gain some benefit. The term is actually a misnomer as it is not inherently possible to steal another person's identity. The person whose "stolen" identity is used by another is a victim and can suffer various consequences when he is held responsible for the perpetrator's actions.

When a person becomes the victim of an offense, it can be as though a part of him stalls at that moment. The person's true identity – being made in the image and likeness of God (Genesis 1:26) – becomes marred. Confusion, anger, bitterness, and desire for retaliation are some common responses to an offense. Having the offense repeated or reinforced often distances a person from a proven antidote: forgiveness. Ultimately, the real thief of identity is the devil. He wants to undermine a person's true identity by disrupting and masking the image of God's original intent and setting the person on a course of self-destruction.

So when the man whose identity as "the paralytic" had his sins forgiven and full mobility instantly restored, it is no wonder as he walked out through the stunned onlookers that they exclaimed, *"We've never seen anything like this before!"* (Mark 2:12) It is appropriate that they also responded by praising God. The man suddenly got his correct identity back by the compassion and power of Jesus Christ, the Son of the Living God! His "issue" would never again be his identity. Forgiveness freed him from the bondage of sin. Jesus' authority redeemed his true self.

Exercising authority

Luke 4 is perhaps one of the clearest chapters in the Bible to illustrate how authority is exercised through the mouth with astonishing results. To begin, Jesus quoted Scripture to end Satan's harassment. At Jesus' command, demons were cast out and infirmities were driven from human bodies. Verse 36 says, *"Amazed, the people exclaimed, 'What authority and power this man's words possess!'"* Jesus exercised his authority both simply and forthrightly. This included forgiving sins.

We are given authority as we come under authority. By humbly submitting to the authority of the Lordship of Jesus Christ, we can demonstrate our blood-covenant right of relationship with him to exercise authority as he did. We, too, can cast out demons and heal the sick in Jesus' Name! We can forgive others and ourselves, proving our authority as Jesus' representatives. On my own, I find it difficult to forgive. But yielding to the authority and power of Jesus' Name makes the otherwise difficult possible.

In 2 Corinthians 2:5-11, Paul helps us understand this cooperation with the Lord in forgiving sins and the benefit of corporate forgiveness. First, he *acknowledges* there is hurt (v5): *"the man who caused all the trouble hurt all of you more than he hurt me."* Next, he comes into *agreement* in expressing forgiveness (v10a): *"When you forgive this man, I forgive him, too."* Paul then asserts his right of *authority* (v10b): *"And when I forgive whatever needs to be forgiven, I do so with Christ's authority for your benefit."* Finally, he emphasizes the *aim* of forgiving (v11): *"so that Satan will not outsmart us. For we are familiar with his evil schemes."*

Do not be deceived to think when an offense occurs that either a person or God is the enemy. Satan is the real enemy and forgiveness is offensive to him!

Elsewhere, Paul instructs us to *"Put on all of God's armor so that you will be able to stand firm against all strategies of the devil"* – including the devices of offense and bitterness. The truth stands: all created things and all created beings submit to the all-authority of the true Lord Jesus Christ. That includes the devil along with *"evil rulers and authorities of the unseen world, mighty powers in this dark world, and evil spirits in the heavenly places."* (See Ephesians 6:11-12) We, too, are submitted to Jesus Christ's all-authority yet in His Name utilize conferred authority to overthrow the real enemy, Satan, and to forgive those who have hurt us – including ourselves.

Be honest enough to admit your anger, bitterness, frustration, disappointment, fears, and other hurts toward the person who has offended you. God is bigger than all of that, including any offense against or anger toward him. Besides, it is not as though there is any secret from God; you may as well expose those feelings so they can be examined and reconciled.

Anger at God always is rooted somewhere else. These feelings may be repressed because the knowledge of being bitter toward God is either too painful or too shameful to admit. Moreover, these feelings may be kept hidden for fear of what others might think.

Deep down inside, some people really believe that God is the one who is to blame for their hurt. They ask, "Why did God allow bad things to happen when he had the power to stop it?" The legitimate question to ask might be, "Why did my parents not protect me?" or "Why did my teacher not defend me?" or "Why was the drunk driver not stopped before the accident?" or "Why did my friends not come to my aid?" Remember, Satan is the real enemy. He wants to divert us from truth and have us lay the blame on God.

Romans 8:28 reveals that *"God causes everything to work together for the good of those who love God and are called according to his purpose for them."* The fact is, bad things that happen really are bad. The truth is, God is able to turn evil into blessing. As for all the bad things that have happened, I simply must affirm that God is God. He is just, and his justice will one day prevail. He knows exactly what he is doing and why. Because he sometimes appears to have been absent or unfair, we may need to surrender our bitterness and forgive God even though he is not guilty.

Forgiveness is at the core of who God is and what he has done through Jesus Christ. As he has done, we are to do. Forgiveness is a supernatural intervention of setting wrongs right. It is a matter of faith and obedience with the ultimate example set by Jesus Christ on the cross. Forgiveness requires both your will – that is, your willingness to forgive – and God's power. May God give you faith to put forgiveness into practice, believing that he, the Lord of forgiveness, has forgiven you and authorizes you to forgive in Jesus' Name.

Prayer pause

Jesus, you know what pain and suffering are all about, yet you forgave those who wrongly accused and ruthlessly abused you. I ask you to go with me to my personal places of pain so I might likewise forgive those who have wounded me. I trust in the power and authority of Your Name to help me forgive others, as you have forgiven me. Amen.

The Law of Forgiveness

The idiom "no strings attached" means there are no obligations or requirements involved. If I make a donation to a charity with no strings attached, the gift can be used by the charity for whatever purpose it chooses.

Forgiveness offered with "no strings attached" aligns with 1 Corinthians 13:5, *"Love ... keeps no record of wrongs."* The unconditional nature of forgiveness means we are not keeping score to use later as "proof" against our offender. We stop blaming and shaming others. Forgiveness is not about being right or initiating revenge. It is about restoring relational order, starting with ourselves. It is about canceling the debt of whatever it is we feel owed by another.

It may surprise you that God attaches strings and places conditions upon forgiveness. Matthew 6:14-15 plainly states, *"If you forgive those who sin against you, your heavenly Father will forgive you. But if you refuse to forgive others, your Father will not forgive your sins."*

This is not some nice suggestion Jesus is making here. It is an imperative.

Jesus' agony on the cross underscores how serious God is about this. Jesus is the epitome of forgiveness, as seen in the prior chapter. Not only did he forgive those who scandalized him, Jesus also took upon himself my sins and yours, forgiving them completely by his shed blood. Since our debt is paid, it is reasonable, in God's view, that we likewise forgive others.

Ephesians 4:31-32 offers two steps of how we are to forgive in light of Jesus' sacrifice and example:

1) *"Get rid of all bitterness, rage, anger, harsh words, and slander, as well as all types of evil behavior."* (v 31) Such behaviors are often indicative that there is unforgiveness on the inside. To abandon such feelings and responses requires some introspection and some self-examination of the heart. It requires discovering where these things are rooted. It will also require some help – which has already been made available to us at the cross.

2) *"Be kind to each other, tenderhearted, forgiving one another, just as God through Christ has forgiven you."* (v 32) It is hard to demonstrate such compassion until bitterness is uprooted and banished. Again, these are not suggestions. We are commanded to forgive because God has forgiven us through the blood sacrifice of Jesus Christ. He provided a way for hostility to be exchanged for kindness.

The requirements of these two verses are non-negotiable. There is not another option. It *is* possible to forgive others, even as we have been forgiven. With God's help, we *can* have a change of heart toward those who have hurt us.

The real reason so many do not forgive is because they want revenge. The best weapon at our disposal to do that is the tongue. We can slander our offender. We can rationalize their just deserves. We can disguise our hurt and anger as merely "getting it off my chest."

But the tongue is also our best weapon for countering our bent toward retaliation. Proverbs 18:21 says, *"The tongue can bring death or life."* Sincere words of forgiveness aptly spoken are life-giving and powerful. They have the capacity to overthrow the enemy's intent to steal, kill, and destroy.

However, we are unable to forgive by our own ability. We need God's help. James is right when he says, *"no one can tame the tongue. It is restless and evil, full of deadly poison. Sometimes it praises our Lord and Father, and sometimes it curses those who have been made in the image of God. Blessing and cursing come pouring out of the same mouth. Surely, my brothers and sisters, this is not right!"* (James 3:8-10) By submitting the tongue to the supernatural power of Jesus, and by exercising our rightful authority in His Name, we can experience the wonder of forgiveness in the natural realm.

Acting nice is not evidence of forgiveness if there has not been a genuine heart change that accompanies sincere expression. Otherwise it becomes just that: acting – a ruse that cannot be sustained long-term.

The reality is, people are going to hurt us, and we are going to hurt others. Paul wrote in Colossians 3:13, *"Make allowance for each other's faults, and forgive anyone who offends you. Remember, the Lord forgave you, so you must forgive others."* Forgiving others starts by considering how much forgiveness God has granted me. Taking stock of this provides me with a sober perspective for considering the faults and failures of others. From this perspective flows decisive and deliberate statements of genuine forgiveness.

Consequence of unforgiveness

Jesus' parable of the unforgiving servant is recorded in Matthew 18:23-35. In brief, a debtor owed a king millions of dollars. When he could not pay, *"his master ordered that he be sold – along with his wife, his children, and everything he owned – to pay the debt."* When the man begged for mercy and patience, *"his master was filled with pity for him, and he released him and forgave his debt."*

Upon leaving the king's presence, he accosted a fellow servant who owed him a few thousand dollars and demanded instant payment. When the fellow servant pleaded for a little more time, his creditor refused. Instead, he had the man arrested and imprisoned until he could pay the debt in full. Some of the other servants who saw this were greatly upset and promptly reported to the king everything that had happened.

"Then the king called in the man he had forgiven and said, 'You evil servant! I forgave you that tremendous debt because you pleaded with me. Shouldn't you have mercy on your fellow servant, just as I had mercy on you?' Then the angry king sent the man to prison to be tortured until he had paid his entire debt."

Jesus punctuates the story with a shocking statement: *"That's what my heavenly Father will do to you if you refuse to forgive your brothers and sisters from your heart."*

In this parable, Jesus teaches that withholding forgiveness and mercy toward another person impedes the flow of God's forgiveness toward us. That's putting it nicely! While God's forgiveness is freely given, nevertheless it remains conditional upon a person's willingness to forgive others. It is as though God is asking, "Do you *really* want my hard-earned forgiveness if you are unwilling to forgive others?"

You see, genuine forgiveness is a heart issue. It transcends intellect, will, and emotions. Forgiveness is also utterly supernatural. It engages me in a truth encounter with the Living God and what he requires of me to be in right relationship with him as well as with those who have wronged me. It feels unnatural and unfair to forgive them. But it is God's way. He loves us enough to have provided a way to both receive and give forgiveness. That way is through Jesus. Because of his love, he forgives us freely and expects us to freely forgive others.

Neither debtor in Jesus' parable could pay his enormous debt. In both cases, immediate settlement of accounts was demanded. In a similar way with those who have in some way hurt us, we want to exact payment. We want to get back what we feel they owe us: love, respect, protection, acceptance, innocence, dignity, truth, time, provision, or something else. In most cases, the chances of ever getting such things back from them are highly improbable.

Finally, accounts can be settled in one of two ways. We can forgive others and release them from their debt to us or we can put them in an impossible situation of demanding something they may be unlikely or unable to pay.

God calls for us to settle accounts his way: by releasing and forgiving as he has done, showing both mercy and grace. Or, we can suffer the consequences of trying to do it our way by exacting retribution. God has already demonstrated the lavish extent of his forgiveness and is willing to work with us to do likewise for others. As we do our part, God will do his – even with one of the hardest people to forgive: yourself.

Forgiving yourself

People who cannot forgive themselves tend to exhibit some common traits. They punish themselves by replaying in their minds their sin or offense toward others. They feel undeserving of forgiveness. They have feelings of guilt or shame for what has happened. All such inclinations are prompted and encouraged by the devil.

Some seek to overcome their guilt by excessive behaviors such as substance abuse, perversions, overindulging, blaming, manipulation, or other abnormal pursuits. They may be seeking solutions to deal with unresolved pain, bitterness, or unforgiveness. All these merely become diversions from addressing the real issue and serve as forms of denial or avoidance. For example, a person may take on multiple jobs at church to prove his dedication but at the same time be avoiding the truth: he is in pain.

On the other end of the spectrum, some may deprive themselves or abstain from good things in life or from pursuing God's best. They may reason that they are no more deserving of good things than they are of forgiveness. This false path of deprivation denies God's grace and also keeps them from confronting their pain.

People who do not forgive themselves tend toward disappointment in themselves, often due to unfulfilled expectations. Some develop a false sense of humility. They find it difficult to accept a compliment from others and feel unworthy before God. The person who has not forgiven himself may find it hard to forgive others.

As a person finds ways to protect himself from going to that place of pain and forgiving himself, he may get lost in a fog of uncertainty. If he has not forgiven himself, he may wonder if God can or will forgive him. In the confusion, he may lose sight of the truth that the blood of Jesus covers all sins and offenses; that God's forgiveness through Jesus is a free gift. It cannot be earned. But like any gift, it can be either accepted or rejected.

Burden bearing

In Chapter One, I shared a definition of offense as "a cause or occasion of sin." Psalm 103:12 says, *"He* (the Lord) *has removed our sins as far from us as the east is from the west."* In verse 13, we learn that the Lord is like a father to his children, tender and compassionate. He is merciful, slow to anger, filled with unfailing love. He does not deal harshly with us, as we deserve. The Lord is willing to remove our sins as well as the offense of those sins. This includes the root of bitterness.

1 Peter 5:7 urges, *"Give all your worries and cares to God, for he cares about you."* Many are burdened by the weight and worry of unresolved pain. A "holy exchange" takes place as the ever-present Lord Jesus comes not only to bear our burdens, but also to bear them away "as far as the east is from the west." He supernaturally exchanges the pain for healing, the lies for truth, the fears for peace.

In Matthew 11:28-29, Jesus said, *"Come to me, all of you who are weary and carry heavy burdens, and I will give you rest. Take my yoke upon you ... and you will find rest for your souls."* To be yoked with Jesus means to go the same pace and rhythm. Jesus wants to teach us how to be in sync with the Father when it comes to being forgiven by him and forgiving others. God's forgiveness leaves no doubt. It is absolute. Final. My sins will not be held against me.

Prayer pause

Heavenly Father, please forgive me my sins even as I forgive those who have sinned against me. Please remove the hurt and pain. Bear my burdens away. Thank you for canceling my debt. Thank you for releasing and forgiving me in Jesus' Name. Amen.

The Lure of Forgiveness

I marvel at the long-term influence a phrase, slogan, or even a line from a movie can have upon a culture. Way back in 1970, the movie "Love Story" pervaded our thinking with one of the most stupid and inaccurate proclamations ever: "Love means never having to say you're sorry." People still believe that today and live accordingly. The devil continues to dupe people by its falsehood. In truth, love means we will address offenses responsibly. Love means we will both give and receive forgiveness.

Forgiveness is not devoid of self-interest. The attraction to forgive could be for some purely selfish reasons! Psalm 103:2-4 extols, *"Praise the Lord, O my soul, and forget not all his benefits – who forgives all your sins and ... redeems your life."* (NIV) The benefits and blessings of God are linked to forgiveness – both God's forgiveness of me and my forgiveness of others. Consider some of the advantages and rewards of forgiveness:

1) Forgivers know first and foremost that God is a forgiver. The primary motivation for forgiving others was elaborated upon in the previous chapter, as found in Matthew 6:14-15: so that God will forgive us. What a relief to know that God forgives! Acts 3:19 tells us to repent and turn to God *"so that your sins may be wiped away."* Because He has forgiven our sins, we have an incentive to forgive others who sin against us.

2) Forgivers are joyful. Romans 4:7-8 quotes Psalm 32:1-2 as saying, *"Oh, what joy for those whose*

disobedience is forgiven ... whose record the Lord has cleared of sin." You can extend that same joy to others when you forgive them and cancel their debt toward you.

3) Forgivers are better givers. Research indicates that they volunteer more, donate more to charity, and generally are more selfless toward others. The converse is true of those who do not forgive.

4) Forgivers are healthier, both physically and emotionally. Studies show that forgiveness lowers heart rate and blood pressure. It contributes to emotional as well as physical healing and wholeness. Forgiveness improves sleep quality, releases stress, lessens fatigue, reduces depression, and relieves both psychological and somatic complaints. It can alleviate resentment, hatred, and sorrow. Forgiveness has been shown to restore positive thoughts, feelings, and behaviors toward the offending party. Forgivers are better conflict managers. These are all desirable benefits for overall health and reason enough to convince people to let go of offenses. But God did not demand that we forgive just so we will feel better.

5) Forgivers experience physical and emotional relief. One astonishing and often uncontrollable thing that happens when a person forgives is a release of pent-up emotion. He may let out an involuntary sigh, experience a flow of tears, or feel as though a weight is lifted.

6) Forgivers offer grace and mercy. Grace is getting what we do not deserve. Mercy is not getting what we do deserve. Grace is demonstrated by

what we choose not to say or do to someone who has wronged us. Withholding information or facts that might otherwise harm your offender's reputation shows mercy, even if you know those things are true. Grace and mercy are counter to society's prevailing attitudes of entitlement and opinion. Forgiveness is about letting go and not letting on about anything that could discredit the other person.

7) Forgivers are free. Sincere expressions of forgiveness help break the power of unforgiveness and oppression. Many who have walked through healing and forgiveness discover that people who formerly wounded them are no longer able to trigger or hurt them. Forgiveness has finally become a settled issue, not as words of the mouth or as an act of the will, but in the depths of both the mind and the heart.

8) Forgivers please God. Perhaps the greatest positive value of forgiving is to know you have obeyed God. He asks us to forgive. When we do, he is pleased.

Comprehensive personal health care includes forgiveness. For our spiritual, physical, mental, emotional, and relational well-being, there may be many other benefits of forgiving others that are not mentioned here.

Love your enemies

Luke 6:27-36 provides insight into the response we are to have toward our enemies. Jesus' teaching includes the instructions to *"Love your enemies, do good to those who hate you, bless those who curse you, pray for those who mistreat you. Do to others as you would have them do to you. Love your enemies ... without expecting to get anything back. Be merciful, just as your Father is merciful."* (NIV)

What is an enemy? An enemy is someone who wants to harm you, ruin your credibility, call your integrity into question, or who will take unfair advantage of you. It may be someone who openly hates you or seeks to injure, dominate, or persecute you. People who have hurt us may be perceived as enemies. They may in fact be people that we need to keep a distance from so they cannot continue to hurt us. Yet we are called to forgive even these.

Not everyone we have to forgive is an enemy. It may be that some have unintentionally hurt us or do not know they have offended us. Sometimes it is harder to forgive those who are *not* our enemies – those to whom we may be the closest. But just as there are benefits to forgiving our enemies, there may actually be benefits to having enemies!

An enemy can show us what we are really made of. David's enemy, Saul, shaped him as a warrior, leader, and strategist. Joseph's brothers unwittingly sold him into an ultimate position of power and authority that preserved the lives of many, including their own. Paul's foes only strengthened his resolve to evangelize, making him even more resilient and determined to spread the gospel far and wide.

Do not be angry with your enemy. The Lord may be using your enemy to shape you into God's image and likeness even as he prepares you to fulfill your destiny. We learn from David that an enemy will keep you on your toes. He will also keep you on your knees as you are compelled to go to the Lord for protection and help. Jesus teaches that God blesses us when we are mocked, persecuted, and lied about. He even has the audacity to say we should be happy about this! Why? Because it leads to a great reward in heaven. (See Matthew 5:11-12) The examples of David, Joseph, Paul, and others suggest rewards on this side of heaven as well.

If a person does not solicit our forgiveness, going to them usually causes more problems than are solved. Eighty to ninety percent of people sincerely believe they have done nothing wrong or, if they did something wrong, believe they were justified. They would be indignant, even defensive, at the suggestion they have hurt you in some way.

If we wait for someone to come to us to ask forgiveness, forgiveness may never happen. God forgave us long before we ever asked for it – even of things for which we may never think to ask forgiveness. Similarly, we can forgive others for things they will never know about.

It is up to me to forgive from the heart all my enemies and those who have offended me. If I do this sincerely, I will not be devastated if there is no reconciliation. If those who hurt me do not want to continue a relationship with me, that is not my problem because I have both forgiven and released them.

The power of forgiveness

Many have been taught to speak forgiveness along these lines: "As an act of my will, I forgive so-and-so." Yet it often happens that when you encounter that person, see his picture, hear his voice on the phone, think of him, or even hear mention of his name, anxiety grips you on the inside. Any reminder might evoke fear and the instinct to escape.

Despite determination to forgive "seventy times seven," this repeated "act of the will" is incompatible with the emotions you try to suppress. This can cause confusion about what forgiveness is supposed to feel like – especially if others utter similar prayers and appear to be fine. To illustrate, I share here an edited account taken from my book, TRADING FACES.

Jen was reluctant to think about Bruce. "Besides, I've forgiven him," she asserted, desperately wanting to believe her words made it so.

Urged to get in touch with her feelings at the mention of Bruce's name, Jen began following the trail of fears and lies strewn along the pathway of her memories. She finally stopped at the recollection of the first time Bruce had fondled her in junior high. "It's my fault I didn't stop him," and "I'm dirty," were pinpointed as two lies linked to that encounter which had been tucked away in her subconscious. Fear, shame, guilt, and confusion mingled with the recollection of pleasure and excitement she also had felt.

Three years later, Bruce robbed Jen of her virginity. "My life is ruined," she concluded. "No one will ever want me now." As Jen thought of and talked about Bruce, hatred and anger reached the boiling point in the cauldron of destructive feelings that had been stirred up.

Even though as an adult Jen had repeatedly forgiven Bruce "as an act of my will," here at the experiential memory level she reconnected with her true feelings. From this surprising perspective as a thirteen-year-old, Jen dropped her head in shame and started to weep. As a young teen, she had no idea what to say or do to resolve the pain. In that context, Jen was introduced to the language of forgiveness. She was coached in how to express forgiveness as she visited various memories where Bruce had hurt her. Jen was then able to receive God's truth and be set free from the bondage of lies she had believed about herself.

Once the doorway of forgiveness is opened, it is not uncommon for a torrent of statements to flood out of a person. Jen's forgiveness inventory became surprisingly long as she moved from memory to memory and found there were more individuals than just Bruce who had deeply hurt her. She even realized how she had hurt herself.

After some time, Jen could not think of one more statement to make. The mental exercise she had been through was exhausting. Sinking back into her chair, she said, "I feel as though a huge weight has been lifted off me." At her next session, Jen was able to report that an intervening chance encounter with Bruce had not triggered any ill feelings. Quite the opposite: she found she felt sorry for him. Jen was able to look upon him for the first time with compassion as a person who was also wounded.

Declarations of forgiveness are extraordinarily liberating. Jen discovered two ways that can also help *you* know that forgiveness has taken place. First, negative feelings finally disappear. You will not feel the same way the next time you see or are reminded of that person. Former feelings of resentment may now be replaced with compassion. Second, it is easier to accept the person because there is understanding. Understanding does not excuse what others did to you, although forgiving them changes your perspective. Genuine concern for another's well-being overshadows any desire for retaliation.

God's way of forgiveness is in a category all its own. It not how the world operates and it defies our human tendencies. Perhaps the only thing harder than forgiving is not forgiving.

Prayer pause

Heavenly Father, I value intimacy with you more than I desire to see my enemies punished. Thank you for treating me according to what I need and not as I deserve. Help me to treat others the same way. Amen.

The Language of Forgiveness

I was raised on a farm in far northwestern Minnesota where the frost line could penetrate six feet into the earth. This contributed to a strange phenomenon as the earth began to thaw in the Spring. Things that were buried, like rocks, would be forced to the surface. Each year, we would criss-cross our 2,500 acres with a tractor to pick up varying sized rocks that had not been there the year before! These would be thrown onto a low trailer then added to existing piles where rocks had been discarded from previous years. Had this exercise not been done annually, the rocks could damage farm equipment, resulting in costly repairs and delays.

As a person begins warming up to the idea of forgiving someone, it may be like those rocks in the fields during a Minnesota thaw: a certain circumstance in life might force the "rocks" of hurt to the surface so they can be removed once and for all. But that takes work and invariably involves others.

It is said that hurting people hurt people. Those who exhibit characteristics such as bitterness, negativity, complaint, or anger are often hurting on the inside. Unfortunately, many simply have no skills to reverse the hurt. Therefore, when people are wounded, several unsatisfactory responses occur:

1) They nurse the hurt by rehearsing the offense in their conscious mind, maybe even strategizing revenge. In so doing, they are also reinforcing the hurt in their subconscious mind. Both contribute to nourishing a root of bitterness.

2) They find ways to dissociate, or separate, from the pain (or the person who caused it) in order to protect themselves from being hurt again.

3) They seek solutions to salve or hide their pain. Astonishingly, such solutions may present themselves as all manner of addictive behaviors, destructive tendencies, and even falling into other damaging relationships.

4) They deliberately pursue revenge and look for ways to hurt back the one who has hurt them.

"Time heals all wounds" is a misnomer. Most counselees admit that staving off forgiveness usually only makes things worse. To trust in time to deal with offenses is a copout to expressing forgiveness. Time is not the healer. God is the healer, even though sometimes healing takes time.

I wish that I could offer you a simple "add water and stir" recipe for addressing unforgiveness. I do not have such a formula, but will share with you four principles I have discovered that, when applied, will set free those captive to bitterness and unforgiveness.

1) *The language of forgiveness*

Before one can speak the language of forgiveness, what is being forgiven must be made clear. Doctors tell us that pain is a good thing. It tells us that something is wrong, whether the pain is physical or emotional. If we do not understand what is at the root of the pain, we will only be treating symptoms and not the cause.

Therefore, it is imperative to get into the context of the hurt at the experiential memory level in order to find healing. This can be achieved by simply asking

God to help you connect with the pain. More specifically, asking him to take you to the place where you were first wounded. The good news is, you do not have to travel to that forbidden place alone. Our ever-present Lord will go with you.

Because God heals in the environment of community and relationship, I strongly urge that you have a trusted friend, pastor, or prayer partner with you as well. Speaking forgiveness in the hearing and agreement of another person strengthens accountability. Your audible expressions will also resonate in the spirit realm. The enemy knows you mean business when there is a witness to these statements.

Maybe you have been led to forgive a past offense in the context of the present. You logically and rationally forgave the person who hurt you, but later discover the pain is still there. That is because until forgiveness is expressed at the heart level and in the context of the pain, you will find neither freedom nor healing.

Hebrews 4:13 says, *"Nothing in all creation is hidden from God."* God already knows what happened. He is waiting there to meet us at the place where we are most vulnerable. By opening up in this way to God and others, you could unexpectedly find yourself in a memory. Maybe it is of the first time you were abused or hurt in some other way. It could be the very place you have blocked out in order to survive. Or, it could be the very thing that has haunted and tormented you for years. Perhaps that place has never been disclosed or discussed before with anyone else. Whatever the case, do your best to transport yourself into the circumstance and the emotional "now" of the memory.

Once there, you might actually feel within yourself as though you are at that age or in that place again.

It is while you are in this context that it is particularly helpful to have "Jesus with skin on" in the form of that trusted confidant. He or she will keep you safe, protect you in your disclosures, and help you get through emotionally hurtful issues.

While there, prepare to engage the language of forgiveness by plainly stating:

"God, I forgive _____ (name the person)

for _____ (identify the offense).*"*

It is necessary to be *specific* and *honest* in your expression. This is not the time to rationalize, justify, or attempt to explain away what happened to you. For example, "Oh, I know that he was hurting as well," or "He didn't really mean to do that." The truth is the truth. Do not minimize the offense or muddle around. Neither make any allowance for "buts": "I forgive him for this, *but* ..." Every time a "but" is included, forgiveness is made conditional. Your friend may be able to assist you and keep you on task.

A few practical considerations while in the context of that place of pain:

1) Ask the Holy Spirit to reveal all unresolved issues.

2) Acknowledge the truth. A part of you may not *want* to forgive this person. Admit that. But at the same time, truthfully confess your *willingness* to forgive. Do not remain in bondage because of unwillingness or inability to forgive.

3) If it helps, visualize the person who has hurt you. Some find it beneficial to sit opposite an

empty chair, or even to place in the chair a pillow or other object that represents that person.

4) Knowing that the person is not really there across from you, express your true feelings. Speak these from the context of the pain, not your present day rationale. Be frank. Be vocal. Be emotional. Let it out! Release those pent-up hurts. Realize, however, that venting your feelings or admitting your hurt does not bring healing.

5) Engage the language of forgiveness for each instance of offense. Be specific. Be honest. Be thorough.

"God, I forgive _____ (name the person)

for _____ (identify the offense)."

Or, you may want to interject the person's name first:

"_____ (name of person),

I forgive you for _____ (state the offense)."

6) Look around in the context of that memory or memories. Is there anyone else you need to forgive? Do you need to forgive yourself for something? Do you need to forgive God? Back up one step and re-engage the language of forgiveness for each one who comes to mind.

7) Some people believe lies about themselves because of what has happened. Maybe, "I deserved this," or "My life is ruined," or "No one could love me now." While there, invite Jesus to reveal the truth to you, however he chooses to do that. Remember, he is ever-present both then and now. He alone can legitimately

dispel all lies because he alone is *"the way, the truth, and the life."* (John 14:6) Logical truth and rational thinking cannot do what only Jesus can do once and for all.

8) Take your time. Do not rush. As the "Jesus with skin on" friend for another, the longest I have listened to a person consecutively speak forgiveness is one hour and forty-five minutes! It is amazing what tumbles out of a person once the doorway of forgiveness is safely opened.

9) Do not push or force this experience. If there is resistance or hesitation, pause. Evaluate whether it is possible to continue at this juncture, or if it is best to return to it at a more opportune time of readiness. In the meantime, it may be helpful to journal your thoughts or process them in some other way before continuing.

10) Ask your friend who is listening to your confessions and statements to pray healing and restoration over you.

After every last statement has been exhausted, people often express as a startling realization, "I thought I had forgiven him!"

2) Renunciations

While expressing forgiveness, it may be that you become aware of generational curses or soul ties that need to be renounced.

A generational curse is a form of involuntary inheritance through the bloodline of lineage and of ancestral sin. These are often determined by their ill effects such as poverty, barrenness, chronic or hereditary infirmity, mental illness, failure, or hindrances in spiritual growth. They might also be recognized as family patterns of such things as adultery, alcoholism, or abuse.

While in the context of the place of pain, speak with confidence when renouncing such curses:

"By blood covenant right of relationship with my Lord, Jesus Christ, I take authority over the enemy, Satan, and the harm he has sought to do directly to me through my ancestry and through others.

"In Jesus' Name, I renounce and reject all generational curses and demonic influences that have come upon me through the bloodline of my lineage. I declare that all ancestral sins and their effects are now revoked and canceled from the beginning of time, to the end of time, to the present. They will not be visited upon my children or my children's children."

A soul tie curse is one acquired through an unrighteous relationship and the corresponding transference of demonic influence from one person to another. This can occur through a range of relational connections including generational inheritance, illegitimate sexual union, occult connections, abuse, and trauma. Speak boldly to these as well:

"In the Name of Jesus and by his blood, I break all unrighteous soul ties that are unholy, ungodly, unnatural, illegitimate, perverse, and demonic. I renounce the soul tie curse of any and all illegitimate sexual relationships or one-flesh bonds experienced in the physical body, or vicariously through pornography, fantasy, or perverse dreams.

"I renounce, declaring null and void, all such soul ties between me and (name of person) and between (same person's name) and me. I send back to (name of person) all portions of his soul that have been unrighteously deposited in my humanity. I call back to myself all fragments of my soul that have been taken from me by (name of person).

"Thank you, Lord, for restoring my soul and sanctifying my spirit. I ask that only wholesome, holy, and righteous soul ties connect me with others and others with me. Grant me your wisdom and protection in forming relationships. May I live in relational purity and in ways that bring honor and glory to your Name."

3) *Canceling debts*

Once forgiveness has been sincerely expressed and all curses and soul ties renounced, the next step is to cancel all debts of what you are due. Begin by asking the Lord to open up any places where you feel owed and to identify exactly what those debts are.

It may be helpful to create an inventory of who owes you what. The "who" will be those who hurt you. This list might include those who were meant to bring the most love, security, or protection but who did not: parents, relatives, close friends, or people in authority. The "what" lists what was done against you and what you feel owed. For example, perhaps you were bullied. You were robbed of, and therefore feel owed, dignity, self-esteem, and respect. The humiliation made you feel shamed and powerless. You may have wrongly concluded, "I'm a failure" or "I'm a wimp." On the inside, all of that still hurts. Emotional cues tell you that these matters are still not resolved.

Your account might include being owed love and affirmation, security, or provision. Maybe you have suffered poor mental or physical health because of what happened and you feel deprived of well-being and stability. Perhaps an abuse has left you relationally void, spiritually weak, or in some other way cheated. If you feel owed in the least, there is an account to settle. Be truthful and clear with your inventory. Bundle up the hostility and surrender it to Jesus, who taught us to pray, *"Forgive us our debts, as we forgive our debtors."* (Matthew 6:12, NKJV)

Face all shattered expectations and the improbability of ever being paid what the offender truly owes you. A synopsis of Luke 6:35-37 instructs, *"… do not judge … do not condemn … forgive others, and you will be forgiven."* That word typically translated as "forgive" is the Greek "apoluo," which also means "pardon" or "release." To comprehend that passage more fully, you not only forgive a person, you also pardon and release him – which will likewise be done for you. In context, verse 38 further reinforces the principle of sowing and reaping. If you sow forgiveness and cancel all debt, this is what you can expect to reap.

A debt is forgiven when you free your debtor of his obligation to pay back what he owes you. Using your inventory, systematically state and cancel each debt once and for all. Let your debtor go! This is what the king did in Matthew 18: he began with a detailed account of all the servant owed him that could not possibly be repaid. He then settled the account by canceling the enormous debt owed by the servant.

4) *Blessing*

Every aspect of the language of forgiveness is counterintuitive to our nature. That includes this final step, blessing the person who has hurt you. If settling an account cancels debt, pronouncing a blessing might be thought of as writing a big check! You not only free your offender but also offer them something else "they don't deserve": a blessing.

In the process of engaging the language of forgiveness, it may be that you experience genuine empathy for the person who has hurt you. To bless him becomes an apt response. Of our persecutors, Paul insists we are to *"pray that God will bless them."* (Romans 12:14) In accordance with Luke 6:28, we are to bless and pray for those who have mistreated us. If the shoe were put on the other foot, you would not object if someone you had hurt prayed for your well-being, prosperity, and other blessings. And who knows? It could be that you experience certain blessings because someone you have offended has forgiven and prayed this way for you.

The Lifestyle of Forgiveness

All need forgiveness and need to forgive. None are exempt. Forgiveness is at the core of who we are and what we do as Christ-followers. On the cross, Jesus paid the supreme price for the forgiveness of our sins. Therefore, it should not be touted as costly or too difficult for us. We are not the ones who were put on the cross or who paid that price. One aspect of moving toward creating a culture of forgiveness is by moving away from the notion that it is so difficult a thing to do. Forgiveness is meant to be a familiar expression and common activity among us.

We must stop perpetuating the mentality that forgiveness is hard work and will always be so. When I first added stair climbing to my exercise routine, I was puffing and wheezing and sweating profusely after only a few flights. The next morning, I could barely walk because unconditioned muscles that had been overextended were protesting. It was not easy to press on! But I persisted. I paced myself, adding flights incrementally. The more I extended myself, the easier it became. Now I can practically sprint up numerous flights of stairs and back down and barely break a sweat. Why? Because tenacity and practice eventually made it almost second nature to tackle a stairwell. In a similar way, exercising forgiveness will stretch us. It will challenge us. It will be hard work *at first*. There are times we will not want to do it. But perseverance will pay off. Like anything else we practice, we progress in comfort and confidence as we continue to do it.

Too many stay in bondage because they have no idea what to do or what to say in order to deal responsibly and redemptively with past hurts. They have been neither exposed to nor coached in the language and lifestyle of forgiveness. Mentors are needed to help restore order in this area by demonstrating that, with practice, the ability to forgive becomes easier with each opportunity.

Forgiveness education

Exposure to poverty, prejudice, and violence puts children at increased risk of emotional problems such as depression, anxiety, low self-esteem, and disproportionate anger. Forgiveness education is being implemented in places like Northern Ireland, where generations of Catholics and Protestants pass down painful memories of injustice, and in Milwaukee, Wisconsin, a segregated city with a murder rate higher than that of Belfast.

Research has found that children exposed to forgiveness education can learn to respond to injustice and tragedy in a forgiving way, thus refusing to let anger and resentment prevail. Results indicate significant decreases in levels of anger leading to fewer emotional troubles. Meanwhile, building forgiveness muscle over time lends itself to improvements in self-esteem, academic achievement, and more peaceful social behavior. Furthermore, emotional health improvements are sustained, resulting in psychologically healthy adults.

It is admirable for secular education programs to aspire to change a cultural mindset through teaching forgiveness. It is noble that the Amish community's response of forgiveness caused our nation to pause in awe for a moment and consider how that could be.

Yet these actions are deemed unusual and newsworthy rather than the norm.

As believers, we of all people should exude forgiveness by the very nature of who we are. However, it may take deliberately integrating forgiveness education into our lives to help the world see there is something deeper than just emotional or social benefits to forgiveness. We contribute a spiritual component that is unlikely to be presented in schools or to communities. Biblical truths about forgiveness can help combat revenge-based cycles of pain. Such education will bring realignment with God's priorities for all mankind.

Insufficient skills regarding forgiveness could be merely the lack of opportunities either to offer or receive forgiveness. Catholics are provided a regular occasion to receive forgiveness through a confessional box. Rather than go to another believer, they visit a priest in an enclosed stall divided by a screen. Here individuals confess their sins to the priest and seek absolution, or forgiveness, from him. One reason people do this is because they not only want help but also anonymity due to issues such as fear or shame. But many go simply because there is an opportunity provided – a time and a place – to deal with sins and offenses.

Opportunities and invitations to deal with hurts, bitterness, and unforgiveness need not be limited to Catholics, a priest, and a confessional box. Everyone should have the right both to express and experience forgiveness, to know the corresponding release of freedom and healing, and to retrieve their true identity. Ultimately, that right is available because of the blood sacrifice of Jesus Christ on the cross and our coming into saving relationship with him. His forgiveness demands we forgive.

Living and teaching forgiveness as a lifestyle means it can be imparted to others both by example and intention. Many simply have no role model, motivation, or vocabulary for expressing forgiveness. They need both to be taught and to have demonstrated what to do or say, and then allowed personal expression to come forth as they gain confidence. With practice, the discipline of forgiving others will be called upon at the time of offense, thus intercepting the enemy's hope of destroying relationships through bitterness, anger, hatred, and retaliation.

Realistically, in some cases forgiveness takes time. The hurt may be so deep that it takes a while to differentiate the complexity of issues and emotions before the forgiveness process can even begin. Coming to terms with the depth of pain may precede the ability or willingness to express forgiveness at the experiential memory level. However, not all offenses are that complicated, so whenever it is possible, forgive hurts quickly to prohibit Satan's access. Ephesians 4:26-27 urges, *"Don't let the sun go down while you are still angry, for anger gives a foothold to the devil."* Although for the harder cases, realize the sun could rise and set many times before the process of forgiveness is complete. The process may be painful, but like marinated meat, the end result is tender and very appealing.

Lifestyle of forgiveness

Because Satan wants to get his foot in the door as early in life as possible, how much better to start forgiveness education with the young. We cannot risk perpetuating the typical ways of dealing with hurt, which are to treat your offender with contempt, make him pay, alienate him, or teach him a lesson. These customary ways do not make those ways right. By contrast, all who develop and practice a lifestyle of forgiveness will exhibit characteristics that include:

1) Authenticity. The essence of credible Christianity is found in a lifestyle of forgiveness. People who seek this attribute in Christians deserve to find it.

2) Strength. Mahatma Gandhi said it well, "The weak can never forgive. Forgiveness is the attribute of the strong."

3) Reality. Forgiveness is being aware of and acknowledging what a person has done to hurt you and not masking the truth with denial, avoidance, justification, excuses, or seeking revenge.

4) Boldness. We are not designed to control the pain and hurt. Self-effort in itself is not sustainable. Rather, boldness helps us to confront the pain and to forgive.

5) Mercy and Grace. From a strictly human viewpoint, my offender does not deserve forgiveness, but then neither do I deserve God's forgiveness. Nonetheless, I must be willing to give what I have received: both mercy and grace.

6) Genuine freedom. Because Jesus is integral to the power and process of forgiveness, *"if the Son sets you free, you are truly free."* (John 8:36)

It does not seem natural to forgive, desire reconciliation, or to bless offenders, yet it should be the most natural thing we do. The more we practice forgiveness, the harder it is to practice unforgiveness and the more likely it becomes to respond in forgiveness than in offense. True forgiveness is transformational. As you become comfortable with the language of forgiveness you will be more inclined and prepared to confront offenses as they occur. As well, you will provide a role model to others that will pass on a legacy for the future.

Wisdom, discipline, and prayer

Wisdom can be thought of as "seeing things from God's perspective." Wisdom helps us understand how Jesus feels about the person who has hurt us as well as the circumstance of what that person has done. Developing both the wisdom and discipline to exercise forgiveness is part of the process. Incorporating prayer into that process:

1) invites God to show you how he sees the person who has offended you.

2) allows God to transform your mind and heart so that your thoughts and words toward an offender come from God's point of view instead of your own.

3) encourages honesty about confessing the ugliest emotions hidden at the core of your being.

4) stimulates a genuine empathy for the one who has hurt you without excusing what he did.

When I yield my pain to Jesus and pray for those who have hurt me, God's Spirit responds to my small act of obedience by moving in my heart to free me from the grip of bitterness and the desire for revenge. Besides, praying for someone makes it much harder to stay mad and nurse a grudge.

Prayer pause: Thanksgiving

We forgive in order to experience the mystery of being cleansed by God from all unrighteousness, bitterness, and the hurt caused by others. Offering that freedom to others pleases our heavenly Father.

Whenever the Lord does something for us, it is appropriate to give him thanks. Pause to do that right now. Acknowledge God's forgiveness. Celebrate his grace and mercy! Rejoice over the release from debt! Express newfound freedom! Use the following prayer prompts to get you started:

Heavenly Father,

> I acknowledge …
>
> I celebrate …
>
> I rejoice …
>
> I thank you …
>
> I praise you …

Hallelujah and Amen!

Scripture References

Genesis 1:26
Deuteronomy 32:35
Psalm 32:1-2
Psalm 103:2-4
Psalm 103:12-13
Proverbs 18:21
Matthew 5:4
Matthew 5:11-12
Matthew 6:14-15
Matthew 9:1-8
Matthew 11:28-29
Matthew 18:23-35
Mark 2:12
Mark 6:1-6
Luke 4:14-30
Luke 4:36
Luke 6:27-36
Luke 6:35-37
Luke 17:3

Luke 23:34
John 14:6
John 8:36
Romans 4:7-8
Romans 8:28
Romans 12:14
Romans 12:19
Romans 13:8
1 Corinthians 13:5
2 Corinthians 2:5-11
Ephesians 4:26-27
Ephesians 4:31-32
Ephesians 6:11-12
Colossians 3:13
Hebrews 4:13
Hebrews 8:12
Hebrews 12:15
James 3:8-10
1 Peter 5:7

Do you struggle with "another side of yourself" that shows up at inopportune times, unpredictably, even against your will? Or, perhaps you may live or work with someone who acts one way here, another way there, and a completely different way somewhere else. How does this happen? What flips the switch that causes a person to "trade faces" and "become someone else?"

TRADING FACES has answers for you!

Most people are completely unaware of what is really behind the unexplainable behaviors they encounter in themselves or in others on a daily basis. TRADING FACES explores the mystery and perplexity of living both in and with dissociation. This book provides persuasive evidence that dissociation is more than just "split personalities." Learn truths about this phenomenon that separates people within themselves and from others – including God. Then discover the power of inner healing that restores order and puts things back the way they were intended to be.

Doris M Wagner, co-founder of the International Society of Deliverance Ministers endorses TRADING FACES as:

"one of the most clear, concise presentations on dissociation I have found."

For more information about TRADING FACES or Inner Healing Prayer Ministry, visit: www.oikosnetwork.com

Made in the USA